Pumpkin

THE RACCOON WHO
THOUGHT SHE WAS A DOG

Pumpkin

THE RACCOON WHO THOUGHT SHE WAS A DOG

Laura Young

B🌿XTREE

First published in the US 2016 by St. Martin's Press

First published in the UK 2016 by Boxtree
an imprint of Pan Macmillan
20 New Wharf Road, London N1 9RR
Associated companies throughout the world
www.panmacmillan.com

ISBN 978-0-7522-6611-4

1 3 5 7 9 8 6 4 2

A CIP catalogue record for this book is available from the British Library.

Printed in China

For my parents,
Rosie and Peter

Acknowledgments

This book is a dream come true and it would not have been possible without the many wonderful people who have helped and been dedicated to our little Pumps, Toffee, and Oreo.

To my amazing parents, Peter and Rosie, for caring and nurturing our fur children. Mum, we wouldn't be able to do half the things we do without you. Dad, thank you for turning every insect, mammal, or reptile into a "George."

Kyle, thank you for being Pumpkin's social media guru and for always listening to constant tales of our furry bandit!

Edward, thank you for staying up late and helping me make edits to all of the photos. Who else could I have called at ten at night to help calm my nerves!

Steven and Hayley, thank you for always being so patient with the constant Pumpkin chat! Celine, that goes for you too. And for sharing Kyle when things "Hit the fan!" and for listening to my constant worries!

Alexis, thank you for giving me the confidence to follow my passions and for always supporting me.

Gilly, thank you for looking after our little Pumps during the first few days of her new life, and to Molly, for giving her that lovely name.

Kim Aranha, thank you so much for being a part of the book, and for everything you do for the Bahamas Humane Society, and for the animals in the Bahamas!

Sam and Leean from Lovesniffy's, thank you for always supplying Pumpkin with the most delectable treats!

Thank you, Alex Cortani, for all your help with the Web development and designs.

To the wonderful people at the Dodo, thank you for sharing Pumpkin's story. You helped take us on this incredible journey!

Alex Slater, thank you for being an amazing support through this whole crazy journey. You have been above and beyond from day one!

Alicia Clancy, thanks to you and the whole team at St. Martin's Press for being so patient and kind throughout the whole process of creating this fantastic book.

To the incredible fans of Pumpkin, you are the most supportive and loyal friends to our three girls. None of this would have been possible without you, and I will forever be grateful for your kindness and love that you bring my family and me.

And to my amazing husband, Will. Thank you for being the most kind and patient man. What an adventure we have with our three furry girls! I love you!

Introduction

This is the story of an orphaned Bahamian raccoon called Pumpkin and her two best friends, Toffee and Oreo. Pumpkin is an island girl through and through but, unlike her wild cousins, she prefers to remain indoors. She enjoys air-conditioning, leftover tea every now and then, and feasting away on sunny-side up eggs. Her story is unique because not only does she reside in the Bahamas, but she also has decided to make Toffee and Oreo her lifelong friends, her sisters, mothers even.

Toffee and Oreo are dogs, "potcakes," to be precise, a Bahamian term used to describe "mutts." No one really knows why they are called potcakes, and there are many different theories, mine being that they would eat leftover local Johnnycake bread from the pot. My husband, Will, and I found these two sisters on the side of the road when they were only eight weeks old. They had a rough start into the world and were in horrendous condition. Toffee had been hit by a car and had sustained a broken hip and a shattered knee, while Oreo had been badly beaten. We knew instantly that they were meant to be with us and we did everything we could to get them healthy and happy. It wasn't long before the two settled into their comfortable new lives, and they are now the madams of the house.

Pumpkin came along nearly six years later, in October 2014, after a very unusually windy week in the Bahamas. The little raccoon fell out of a tree in my parents', Rosie and Peter's, backyard when she was only one month old and suffered a broken leg. When the mother didn't return, every effort was made to ensure that the tiny creature would have a fighting chance. With the help of friends and vets, we took her in.

In the first few days of her new life, she lived with a family that had cared for injured raccoons before, and that is where a little girl called Molly thoughtfully named her Pumpkin. We never looked back.

Every day Pumpkin grew stronger and braver, and when she met Toffee and Oreo, they developed an instant bond. The dogs watched over and protected her, and it wasn't long before Pumpkin began to follow her two new friends everywhere, never wanting to leave their sides. It was a surprise to all of us to see these three misfits form such a beautiful connection.

Oreo is like the mother, cuddling her and scolding her when she has had enough of Pumpkin's bad behavior. She babied Pumpkin from the start and even tried to nurse her at one stage. Toffee always wants to run around with her or dig her out from under the covers of our bed when she has burrowed. Pumpkin began to act more and more like a dog with each passing day, preferring to stay on the ground like her sisters and copying everything else that they did! They are three very special animals, and I smile every day now that we are a family.

Never in my wildest dreams did I imagine that people would take to Pumpkin and her daily adventures the way they have. I started posting pictures on Instagram as a way for friends and family to follow her progress and see how well she was fitting in at her new home. It has been exciting and eye-opening to see her character develop and her bond with the two dogs grows stronger each day. What makes her little story so special is the way that these unlikely friends have formed an incredible relationship, and it shows that you can find love in the most unexpected places.

Channeling my inner Simba.

My hope is that you read this book and it gives you the warmth and happiness that it gave me to put all of my favorite pictures of Pumpkin, Toffee, and Oreo together. I hope that you are able to take away the following:

At the end of the day we aren't so different from each other, and if a raccoon and two dogs can become friends, then we, too, can have compassion and love for anyone, no matter how different they may seem.

When Pumpkin first came into our lives we were, of course, very nervous about introducing her to the dogs. We did not think it would work and were sure it was going to be a disaster. The moment Oreo saw Pumpkin, she instantly connected with the orphaned baby and decided that she was hers. Toffee was also thrilled. I can imagine her thinking, A new play toy! It took her a little longer to realize how delicate Pumpkin was, but soon the incredible friendship began. Toffee no longer saw her as a toy, but as her new sidekick, and now they are always playing happily together, whether it is Pumpkin pouncing on her, chasing after her tail, or Toffee nudging Pumpkin from under the covers to play outside. They have an unbreakable bond and it is truly heartwarming to see.

Wait, wait, WAIT! Don't sit here!!!!!

I LOVE BISCOTTI!

Going in for the sneak attack!

Oh, the glory! What a delightful little egg!

Humans, the best and only way to travel.

PUMPKIN:

"There, there, Toffee. . . there, there."

TOFFEE:

"What are you doing?"

PUMPKIN:

"Comforting you, silly!"

TOFFEE:

"Why?"

PUMPKIN:

"Because you're going to be sad when
you find out that I ate your treat!"

Toffee...
you
snore too
much!

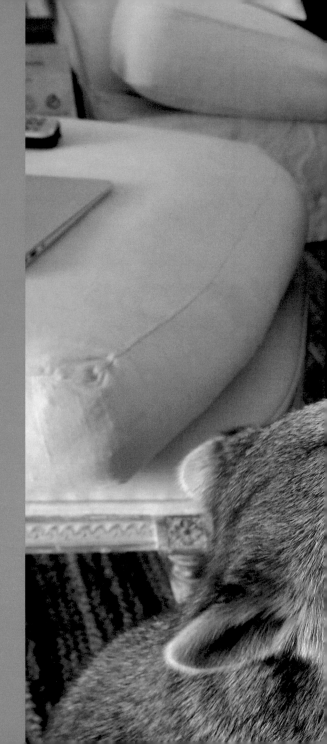

Toffee,
quit
squirming!
You said we
could play
dentist!

Guys, she lied… it's broccoli!

Oreo, I know I'm beautiful,
but didn't anyone ever tell you
staring was rude?

This is my post–peanut butter face.

One of the most frequent questions we get asked is, where does Pumpkin go to the bathroom? When Pumpkin was very young, we tried many different options: kitty litter, taking her outside, but nothing was working. The vet suggested we put her near some water because in the wild that is their preferred place to do their business! It worked, and the goal was to have a space for her outside where she could relieve herself!

One day, I was brushing my teeth and Pumps was playing with the water in the toilet bowl. All of a sudden she was very quiet, and when I looked over to see why she was suddenly behaving, I had to do a double take. There was Pumpkin, squatting down, peeing, staring at me like a child wanting to know if she was doing a good job! She jumped off and, with my toothbrush still hanging out of my mouth, I flushed the toilet as she casually strolled away, and that was that!

We would love it if she could figure out how to flush, but we don't want to get too picky!

Excuse me, sir,
do you have these in
a smaller size?

Stay still, Pumps.
I'm trying to see if I can
fit your whole head
in my mouth!

Oh, boy! That's a lot of pizza!

I'm just checking to see if it's hot, I promise!

Well, maybe just . . .
one . . . little . . . bite . . .

Busted!

Make
sure you
get my
good side!

OREO: "Do you think you should be having that coconut this early?"

Aren't

Make
sure you
get my
good side!

Aren't snuggles just the best?

Don't mind me,
just going to have a power nap
. . . I'll be ready to party in five!

Tag! You're it!

he face of innocence . . . or is it? I want to share a story with you. It is an epic tale and it is known in our house as the Great Flood of Pumpkin. One morning, my husband woke up and made a comment about the rug being wet. I moaned, agitated that he had ruined my peaceful sleep, and grunted, saying that one of the dogs must have peed. What a nightmare! Will quickly replied, "I don't think this is pee. . . ." and wandered out of our room. He then started screaming for me from our living room and I reluctantly pulled myself out of the comfort of my bed. When I put my feet on the ground, I was surprised to find I was standing in a giant puddle. *Great! We have a burst pipe!* was my first thought, and I rushed into the living room to find it covered by at least half an inch of water! Our carpets were soaked through, our sofa's skirts were drenched, and anything that was left haphazardly on the floor was a soggy mess. Will and I both looked at each other and instantly ran to the bathroom where our darling little Pumpkin had been sleeping. There, we found her playing delightfully in pools of water, having the time of her

Living on the edge.

life while the faucet ran a slow, steady stream over the countertop and down to the floor.

I quickly turned off the water and scooped her up, worried that she was in distress. We soon realized that our cheeky little raccoon had figured out how to turn on the tap to play with the water. I inspected the state of the bathroom, which now resembled an indoor swimming pool, but was relieved to see that she had dry refuge in the bathtub. After fussing over her to make sure she was toasty and warm I placed her down, only to have her immediately run to jump in the puddles scattered everywhere. Will and I set to work, trying to extract our soaking-wet furniture and rugs while Pumpkin splashed about happily. She seemed to get such joy observing us as we mopped and toweled down the house, and would use her little hands to try to grab the mop tendrils, making our job that much harder. I kept imagining her thinking how boring we must be because we were *Taking away all my fun! I wanted a pool party!* Will and I found ourselves laughing hysterically, because who does this happen to? People who have raccoons, that's who!

PUMPKIN: "Pumpkin sneaks along, stalking her prey, a silent predator, waiting for the right moment to pounce!"

OREO: "Oh, for goodness sake, Pumpkin, quit being so dramatic and just eat the almond!"

I have an idea!

Today was a good day.
I ate, I slept, I played with my
chew toy, I ate some more . . .
Yup, today was good. I think
I deserve another nap!

Toffee, don't move!
This is the perfect angle to watch the movie!

Mama, these fish don't seem very scared of me!

Oreo? Can you make
my head feel better?

OREO: "Do you think you should be having that coconut this early?"

PUMPKIN: "You know what I always say! It's five o'clock somewhere!"

Oh, yeah! It's cake time!

I am going to be honest with you. Never in a million years did I ever think I would be a mum to a raccoon. When Pumpkin first came into our lives, we were desperate to find her another home, but there were no other options. My husband and I were intimidated, to say the least, but we took it one day at a time, listening to the guidance of friends and vets. Every day, her character would come out and we fell more and more in love with the little rascal, and now she has literally taken over our lives. Everything has had to shift for us to ensure that she is comfortable. She has her own bathroom, and we have had to give up part of our closet because Pumps has decided that it's actually hers. Anything she needs, we adapt to keep her happy and comfortable. To say she is spoiled is an understatement! Pumpkin has brought a lot of changes for us but we would not have it any other way. She has taught us so much and we really cannot imagine life without her. Happy Birthday, Pumpkin! You are a hysterical little gem whom we adore!

Hey, look! I'm a
Pumpkin sandwich!
Get it?

PUMPKIN: "Toffee, did you hide my treat under here?"

TOFFEE: "Nope . . . I ate it."

Squad goals! Even Taylor
would be jealous.

Excuse me . . . have you seen Toffee and Oreo?

I don't know . . . you really don't look like Toffee to me!

I really
thought
this spot
would be
more
comfy!

Plotting world domination . . .
but, first . . . I need snacks!

PUMPKIN: "What do you wanna talk about, Oreo?"

OREO: "It's a little hard to talk when you have your paw up my nose!"

PUMPKIN: "Oh boy, did Mama leave us a treat?"

TOFFEE: "I wouldn't eat that if I were you!"

PUMPKIN: "Why not? It might taste good!"

So, you're saying I can't climb this particular tree? But Mama, it glows!!!!

*P*umpkin has never taken to climbing. When she was younger, and her leg had healed, we would try to teach her the tricks of the trade. At one point, I even began to climb trees in hopes she would follow me! It wasn't very successful because, instead of climbing, she would slide down as fast as she could and continue to follow Toffee and Oreo around! Will and I would get the two dogs to sit beside the tree and we would wait and wait to see if the tree inspired her. It did not.

One day she did decide to go up but, unfortunately, got stuck and froze. My husband had to be the hero of the day and rescue her! That was her last tree-climbing attempt!

PUMPKIN: "Toffee . . . am I doing these sit-ups correctly? I am trying to work off the Christmas pudding!"

TOFFEE: "How much of it did you eat?"

PUMPKIN: "How many would I have to do if, say, hypothetically, I ate . . . all of it?"

Breakfast is always better with a view.

Polite little raccoons
always write their
thank-you cards!

OREO: "We aren't doing anything naughty . . . we swear!"

PUMPKIN: "Speak for yourself!"

Coffee!
Must . .
have . . .
coffee!

Why are we both in a time-out?
Teddy started it.

PUMPKIN: *"Peeeeeeew!* What's that smell?"

OREO: "Don't look at me!"

Maybe she's born with it . . .

But Mama, you said I had to
wash my hands before dinner!

I really don't get the big deal
about New Year's.

Hey, Toffee, think
I could balance a
champagne glass
back there?

To say that Pumpkin loves food is an understatement. She is completely and utterly obsessed with it! That is one instinct that has very much stayed intact for this raccoon-dog! When we first starting getting Pumpkin to eat solid foods, the vet recommended we incorporate eggs somehow. He suggested we give her a boiled egg to get her used to the idea, because they love to play with them! Well, she was not having it and, for a while, I gave up on the idea. One morning I was making eggs for my husband, Will, and myself when she came into the kitchen with her nose wildly sniffing in the air. She then started trying to crawl up my leg desperately, attempting to get a peek at what I was making. Intrigued, I placed some of my breakfast in her bowl, and that is when her love affair with eggs began. She is beyond addicted to the golden morsel that is the yolk, and lets me know every morning that it is time for breakfast! If she does not get her way, she tries desperately to jump up my legs, chatting away until she gets exactly what she wants. Once she has devoured every single ounce of the egg, she waddles away with a full tummy and does her next favorite thing, sleep.

Mama, the egg
is burning!

Oh, thank goodness!
It's perfect!"

PUMPKIN: "Oreo, did you
know that I can read minds?"

OREO: "Do you have to be
so close to do it?"

Just enjoying some
light reading!

I am the best sous chef ever!

The best part about baking
is I get to lick the bowl!

What do you mean,
"this isn't my tail"?

Hey, Toffee, wake up!
I want to go and play outside!

I don't think they will find
me here! Now I can sleep in
all . . . day . . . long!

You'll always be
our little valentine, Pumpkin!

Oh, what did you get me?

What do you mean,
"I can't fly"?

Aw, man, you mean it's
Monday already?

PUMPKIN:
  "Toffee . . . don't move!"

TOFFEE:
  "Why?"

PUMPKIN:
  "I think I just saw Mama!"

TOFFEE:
  "Why do you care?"

PUMPKIN:
  "Because I stole a cookie and I'm
  hiding it behind you!"

Toffee, hold still! You have something in your eye!

Well, I do
declare!

One of the sweetest things that I've noticed about Pumpkin's relationship with the dogs is how much she misses them when they are gone. Every morning when I go and get her from where she sleeps, the first thing she does is go and give Oreo and Toffee a hello. She walks up to them and grabs their noses and licks them or gives them a gentle nibble. She does this when they have come back from walks, and if she is up in the cupboard space, she always pops open a door just to see if it is really them. They can never be apart for long, and Toffee and Oreo do the same. If Pumpkin is still sleeping, Toffee goes to the door and sniffs as if saying, "Please wake up!" It is so heartwarming. We love seeing their relationship blossom!

Oreo, promise you'll
always love me?

Always.

Sharing is caring, Toffee.

ALL FOR ME?

Belly rub?

Did you say "dinnertime"?

I think these would look great
in the living room!

What
natural
beauty . . .
just like
me.

So, this is what you
              call a "spa day"!

Are the ducks supposed
to do something?

Pumpkin emerges from the jungle, inching her way
closer and closer to new lands . . . the kitchen!

But Daddy said I could
have some cookies!

Mama, can you read
me a bedtime story,
please?

Psst, don't tell Toffee, but I am about to pounce on her!

Mum put in the tricky blinds.
That won't stop me from conquering them!

Toffee, Mama says if you keep making faces like that,
one day they are going to stick!

If we smile,
will you give us food?

How does that song go? 'Something something wrecking ball'?

Okay, I'll man the
barbecue
while you get
the drinks!

114

I haven't seen your bag,
your blouse,
or your necklace . . .
I promise!

I really don't like this
hat one bit!

It just doesn't go with
my outfit!

Mama, are
you sure a
hurricane
party
is a good
idea?

*H*aving Pumpkin has been an adventure, and every day she entertains us with something new. Will and I love that we are able to share our funny family and see how much joy she brings others. It has been amazing to see how many people around the world that Pumpkin has touched, and we will continue to update and let everyone be a part of her daily antics with her two best friends!

TOFFEE:
"What do you think she's cooking in there?"

OREO:
"Beats me. Who wants to go and investigate?"

PUMPKIN:
"Nah, let's wait it out . . . she always caves and brings it to us!"

Just because *she's* tired doesn't mean
I have to go bed, too . . . right?

I wonder what my odds are
for getting breakfast in bed. . . .

PUMPKIN: "What curious wonders! I say, Toffee, what *doooo* you think they could be?"

TOFFEE: "Oh, goodness. Pumpkin thinks she's in a 1950s movie. Oreo, we've got to cut back on her TV intake."

Sometimes
you have to
just stop and
smell the roses.

Nothing beats the Monday blues
like a fresh coconut!

Please,
Oreo!
Just one
piggyback
ride!

Sweet dreams, Toffee.

PUMPKIN: "Just stare her down, Toffee, she won't suspect a thing!"

TOFFEE: "I think she sees the crumbs around my lips!"

PUMPKIN: "Just keep . . . calm!"

I love you,
Oreo!

Conclusion

My name is Pumpkin. Most people call me Pumpkin the Raccoon, but I don't really know what that means. What is a raccoon, anyway? As far as I can tell, I am just like my sisters, Toffee and Oreo! I have four legs, a tail, two eyes, and a nose with whiskers! I mean, I can do more things than they can. I know how to stand up on my two hind legs, and I like to wash my food, but, to be honest, we aren't so different. I love nothing more than to play, chasing them around, trying to catch their tails and snuggling up next to them on the sofa or on my parents' bed.

When I first came to be with them, I was very young, so I don't remember much. I do remember feeling the warmth of Oreo's fur and the kisses she would give me on my head. I remember Toffee teaching me not to be scared to go outside and play, and I remember gobbling up my bottle that Mama always gave me.

Some of my favorite things to do are sleep, eat, and play. I love to sleep in the cupboard above all my mama's clothes, with the doors open, of course, so that I can see what is going on at all times. For some reason, though, Mama doesn't like it very much. She prefers that I only keep one door open and is always closing the rest behind me. She does this, like, ten times a day! She is always muttering "You naughty little raccoon!" I sometimes like to reach down and take one of her blouses. They feel so soft and I love to play with the things that hold them. They are so much fun to chew on! Perhaps this is why she calls me naughty, whatever that means!

Mama makes the best eggs in the world! Sunny-side up, all mashed up is the best and only way to eat one's eggs. I love them so much. I also

enjoy avocado, papaya, lettuce, and so many other glorious delights! If I have been really good, she lets me drink the last few drops of her tea, but that is only once in a while. She says it's not good for my teeth to have too many sweets.

Toffee and Oreo love to take me outside for adventures. I must admit that I really don't like to be outside very much. In the Bahamas, it is awfully hot and muggy. I have a lot of fur and it is no fun to be out when the sun is shining! Toffee and Oreo like to nudge me outdoors, and we do have fun exploring around the garden. I adore digging up snails and playing with coconuts that have fallen from the trees, and I especially like to dip my paws in the pool, but I am careful not to get too close! I don't want to fall in!

My most favorite thing of all time to do is to be on the sofa with my family. I love to sit with them and listen to them talk, and curl up next to Oreo and Toffee when I am sleepy. Mama always strokes my neck and tummy and, before I know it, I am fast asleep by her side. I always feel so warm and happy when I am with them.

Even though people say that I am not like my sisters or my parents, I choose not to listen to them. They are my family, and I love them and they love me, no matter what or how different I may seem.

Letter from the Bahamas Humane Society

Laura and Will are two amazing animal lovers who have always put themselves in the forefront of helping animals and assisting the Bahamas Humane Society in so many ways.

Little Pumpkin is just one of many wonderful things they have done. However, as president of the Bahamas Humane Society, I would like to remind people that, although Pumpkin the Raccoon is one of the cutest little animals I have ever seen, it is not advisable to try to keep a raccoon as a pet.

A raccoon is not a companion animal and should therefore be accorded the freedom of a wild animal.

Pumpkin's situation was different because she was found injured and abandoned by her mother. She was so little that she had to be bottle fed. When she was strong and well enough to be released, she had already become a "domesticated" pet.

She has formed an unusual bond with her owners' two dogs and clearly she is now the exception, but it is essential that people understand, generally, raccoons are not house pets, but belong in the wild.

We would like to urge people not to try to mimic Pumpkin's domesticated success. If you see raccoons, leave them be. . . .

If you find an injured raccoon and are in an area where there are wildlife centers, please take it there.

KIM ARANHA
President of the Bahamas Humane Society

Bloopers